D0102869

The
Pullman Strike of 1894

by Michael Burgan

Content Adviser: William Adelman, Professor Emeritus,
Institute of Labor and Industrial Relations,
University of Illinois

Reading Adviser: Katie Van Sluys, Ph.D.,
Department of Teacher Education,
DePaul University

Compass Point Books ✦ Minneapolis, Minnesota

Compass Point Books
3109 West 50th Street, #115
Minneapolis, MN 55410

Visit Compass Point Books on the Internet at *www.compasspointbooks.com*
or e-mail your request to *custserv@compasspointbooks.com*

On the cover: At the end of the Pullman Company strike, the first train leaves the Chicago
stockyards with a U.S. Cavalry escort on July 10, 1894.

Editor: Julie Gassman
Page Production: Ashlee Schultz
Photo Researcher: Svetlana Zhurkin
Cartographer: XNR Productions, Inc.
Library Consultant: Kathleen Baxter

Art Director: Jaime Martens
Creative Director: Keith Griffin
Editorial Director: Nick Healy
Managing Editor: Catherine Neitge

Library of Congress Cataloging-in-Publication Data
Burgan, Michael.
  The Pullman strike of 1894 / by Michael Burgan.
     p. cm. — (We the people)
  Includes bibliographical references and index.
  ISBN-13: 978-0-7565-3348-9 (library binding)
  ISBN-10: 0-7565-3348-1 (library binding)
1. Pullman Strike, 1894—Juvenile literature. 2. Strikes and lockouts—Railroads—Juvenile literature.
3. Railroads—History—Juvenile literature. 4. Labor movement—Illinois—Chicago—Juvenile litera-
ture. 5. Pullman, George Mortimer, 1831–1897. I. Title. II. Series.
  HD5325.R121894 B87 2007
  331.892'825230977311—dc22   2007003940

This book was manufactured with paper containing
at least 10 percent post-consumer waste.

TABLE OF CONTENTS

TROUBLE IN CHICAGO

On Independence Day 1894, the residents of Chicago awoke to a startling sight. Nearly 2,000 armed U.S. Army troops had entered the city overnight and were setting up tents. President Grover Cleveland had received reports of riots in the city, and he feared they would spread. He hoped the soldiers would end the violence and keep trains running in

U.S. troops camped in front of the post office in Chicago.

4

and out of Chicago. Instead, the troops stirred the anger of some Chicagoans and residents of nearby towns.

These people included the homeless, criminals, and workers without jobs. They formed mobs that tipped over railcars. Several fires broke out around the railcars, although who set them was uncertain. As one newspaper reported, "The fire leap[ed] along for miles and men and women danc[ed] with frenzy. ... It was a mad scene." Several days passed before the violence finally ended.

The rioting in Chicago was part of a larger battle between workers and George Pullman, president of the Pullman Palace Car Company. The struggle between Pullman and the workers who built his passenger train cars had started the year before, when Pullman lowered wages. At the same time, he refused to lower the rents he charged workers to live in the town of Pullman. He had built this town just outside of Chicago specifically for his company, and most of his workers lived there.

Because of Pullman's actions, the workers decided to

Hundreds of freight cars filled with rotting food were burned in the violence.

go on strike—they would refuse to work until he restored their old wages. The striking workers belonged to the American Railway Union (ARU). Railroad workers from across the United States belonged to the union, which, like other unions, had formed to seek better pay and working conditions for its members. Western and Midwestern ARU members showed their support for the Pullman workers by refusing to handle any train that pulled a Pullman car. This boycott shut down railway service across the country.

The Pullman strike and others before it were part of a larger struggle between labor (the workers) and capital (the people who invested their money in companies). Most workers felt the U.S. government always sided with capital in disputes over wages or working conditions. President Cleveland's decision to send in the troops seemed proof of that.

But the Pullman Strike led some business and political leaders to see that labor often had real concerns. Many Americans realized that workers sometimes had fair complaints about their wages and working conditions. The U.S. government and some large companies began to address these concerns and accept the role of unions. The strike also led some workers to join political parties that promised to do even more to help workers.

Grover Cleveland (1837–1908)

7

A CHANGING NATION

George Pullman was born in 1831 near Buffalo, New York. He grew up on a farm, as most Americans did at the time. His father, who worked mostly as a carpenter, started a business that moved buildings from one spot to another.

As an adult, George Pullman took over the family business. In 1859, he and his brother went to Chicago. They hoped to make money raising hotels and other buildings from harm's way. If situated too low, buildings were often surrounded by a sea of mud when the Chicago River flooded its banks.

Located along Lake Michigan, Chicago was already the major city of the Midwest. Grain and other goods were shipped through Chicago to cities in the east. Its location and importance in trade led Chicago to become a major railroad center, with many railway lines starting and ending there.

The railroad was just a little more than 30 years old when Pullman moved to Chicago. Americans had seen

Chicago was the world's busiest railroad center. About 100 trains arrived and departed each day.

the value of trains for transporting goods and people over their huge nation. By 1860 the country had 30,000 miles (48,000 kilometers) of track. The growth of railroads led to a demand for iron and then steel for trains and tracks. The trains also needed coal to power their steam engines.

The rise of the railroads, mining, and steel plants were signs of a changing economy in the United States. These businesses created new jobs that led people to leave farms for the cities. Immigrants, mostly from Europe, also came to the United States to fill many of these jobs. This change from farming to industry is called the Industrial

Revolution. This revolution made it possible for George Pullman to make a fortune.

Even before reaching Chicago, Pullman had seen how uncomfortable rail travel could be. In Illinois he started a business to make better sleeper cars, which had beds for passengers taking long trips. His sleepers featured expensive woods and fabrics. They appealed to wealthy riders who

After its dedication in 1886, the Statue of Liberty greeted new immigrants as they arrived. From New York, newcomers often traveled to other cities, including Chicago.

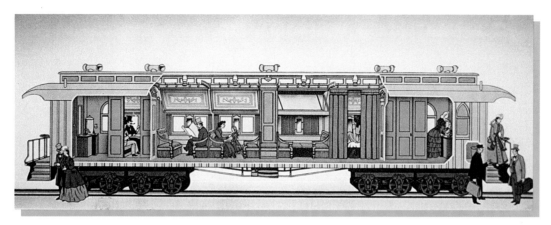

The cost of a Pullman sleeping car was five times as much as a regular rail car.

wanted to travel in comfort. Pullman also designed and built better dining cars and cars where passengers could talk and watch the scenery roll by.

Some historians believe that Pullman's business received a big boost after the death of President Abraham Lincoln in 1865. Pullman convinced the Lincoln family to use one of his cars to transport the president's body to Illinois. Tens of thousands of people saw Pullman cars for the first time, and soon railroad companies were buying or leasing Pullman's cars. In 1867 he opened the Pullman Palace Car Company. The company soon provided jobs to several thousand workers.

BUILDING A TOWN

The Industrial Revolution fueled the growth of cities across the United States. Many were crowded with poor people who struggled to take care of their families. Some immigrants lacked the skills to find jobs. Others could not earn as much as they needed. Even people with decent jobs were often forced to live in crowded, dirty neighborhoods.

New immigrant families often lived in overcrowded one-room apartments.

The poor sometimes turned to crime to survive. And alcohol helped some people forget their troubles.

George Pullman decided he would try to create a town for his workers that would be free from these ills. Happier workers, he believed, would make better workers. Pullman also hoped to keep his workers away from the influence of unions. He believed unions would hurt his business and the United States.

In 1880 Pullman started building a new town on land he purchased just south of Chicago. The new town would enable workers to live close to their jobs. Pullman named the new town for himself, and in 1881 the first residents moved in. Construction continued for several years. Soon Pullman, Illinois, had a library, church, and theater to go along with houses, shops, parks, and a hotel. Most houses had gas, water, and indoor plumbing. Few apartments in Chicago had such conveniences.

In Pullman, workers had modern homes and could easily walk wherever they needed. At the same time, they

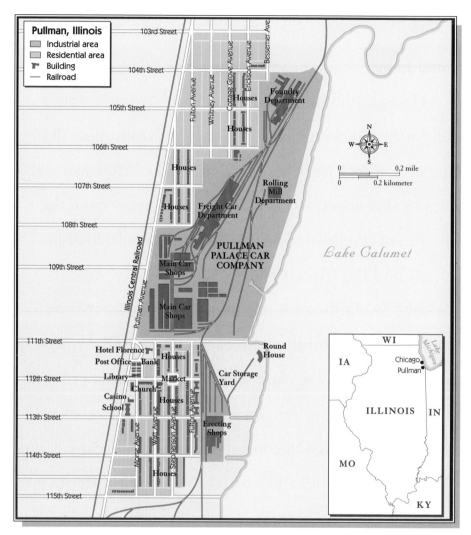

As Chicago grew, the town of Pullman was eventually absorbed into the larger city.

avoided many of the problems found in Chicago and other

big cities. Business and political leaders came to visit and

admire the town. The company boasted that the community

"gives hope of bettering the relations of labor and capital."

Just a few years before, in 1877, the United States had gone through its first violent strike. Railroad workers across the country had left their jobs, seeking better pay. Pullman believed that towns like his would solve workers' problems, and they would no longer see a need to strike.

Pullman's workers, however, were not always happy with life in their new town. Pullman's company controlled all the stores, and it would not let the workers own their homes. Instead, workers paid rent to the company. The rents were higher than those charged in Chicago. The best homes were saved for the company's managers. Pullman expected his workers to keep their homes clean and behave themselves when they left the factory. Workers who did not meet his standards could be kicked out of their homes and their jobs. Pullman alone decided how the town was run. Workers complained that they did not have true freedom, since Pullman had all the power.

A professor named Richard Ely came to Pullman in

15

In Pullman, the homes were mostly brick. They sat along wide streets lined with trees.

1884. The next year, he wrote that the Pullman company's power over the town, "whether … [used] rightfully or wrongfully … is there all the same, and every man, woman, and child is completely at its mercy." Ely called this kind of control over people "un-American" because Pullman residents did not have their full freedoms. Pullman argued that he did not force anyone to work for him or to live in his town. But since he provided better-paying jobs than many other local companies, the workers remained.

UNIONS COME TO PULLMAN

Pullman built a huge factory in his town. Inside the factory, workers sometimes faced unfair conditions. Men called foremen were the bosses of a number of workers. The foremen had the power to hire and fire anyone and set salaries for the workers under them. Workers had no way to complain if they thought foremen treated them unfairly. And if they were fired for causing any kind of trouble, workers' names were sent to other railroad companies. Once these

George Pullman (1831–1897)

workers were on this list of troublemakers, they could not get jobs with other companies. Workers began to dislike the foremen and other managers at the company.

To try to protect their jobs and receive better treatment, many of Pullman's workers joined unions. They used strikes—or the threat of them—to try to improve conditions. Since the company disliked strikes, it fired union members. Remaining union members at the factory had to meet in secret. They often went to bars or clubs in towns outside of Pullman.

Most unions at this time were based on the workers' particular jobs or skills. Carpenters belonged to one union, blacksmiths another, and so on. These distinct unions were called craft unions. About 1,800 Pullman workers also joined the Knights of Labor, which united all the workers in an industry, no matter what job they did. The Knights' leaders said, "An injury to one [worker] is the concern of all."

Many union members believed that all Americans should only work eight hours a day. At the time, most factory workers spent at least 10 hours a day on the job, six days a week. On May 1, 1886, Pullman's Chicago workers took part in a strike to promote the eight-hour workday. Similar strikes took place across the country. Several days later, violence broke out at another Chicago factory, followed by a bomb explosion in Haymarket Square, an area of Chicago. Seven police officers were killed, and eight labor leaders were

The leaders of the Knights of Labor included founder Terence V. Powderly (center).

arrested. The Haymarket Square tragedy, like the Great Strike of 1877, frightened many Americans. They feared the violence that seemed to erupt whenever major strikes

19

Police officers began firing into the crowd at Haymarket Square after a bomb exploded.

occurred. The violence made most business owners and political leaders dislike unions. But many workers believed unions gave them their best chance to improve their working conditions.

20

PROBLEMS OF 1893

In 1893 a huge fair opened several miles north of Pullman in Chicago. The fair was called the Columbian Exposition, and it attracted visitors from around the world. George Pullman had helped bring the fair to Chicago, and the Pullman Palace Car Company proudly displayed some of its railcars. Thousands of the fair's visitors also went to Pullman. A local paper reported that the town was "already

About 27 million people visited the Columbian Exposition during the six months it was open.

famous as one of the wonders of the West."

By the end of the year, however, trouble was stirring in Pullman. When the fair began, the United States was just about to enter a depression. As the economy severely weakened, companies made less money and often fired workers to continue operating. People without jobs often could not pay rent and were forced from their homes. Workers who kept their jobs often saw their wages cut, which made it harder for them to pay bills and feed their families.

The depression of 1893 hit Pullman's company. Railroads stopped ordering new cars, and fewer people rode the Pullman cars already in service. The company made less money than it had, though it still showed a profit. George Pullman wanted to keep the profits as high as possible, so he cut the number of workers by 1,500. The remaining 3,100 workers saw their wages cut by 25 percent to 50 percent. At the same time, however, Pullman refused to lower the rents he charged the workers who lived in his town. He also did not reduce what he paid himself or his top managers.

Name No. 995
Roll No. 40

Pullman's Palace Car Company.
PULLMAN CAR WORKS.
Chicago, Ill.   AUG 31 1893

№ 58015

C

Pullman Loan and Savings Bank,

Pays to the order of   T. Millett $ 0.12

Twelve Cents   **Dollars.**

in full for services to date.   NOT GOOD IF ISSUED FOR A GREATER
AMOUNT THAN ONE HUNDRED DOLLARS

Secretary.   Paymaster.

After rent and utilities were deducted from paychecks, they were not worth more than a few cents.

On June 20, 1893, a group of railroad workers met in Chicago. They formed the American Railway Union (ARU) to unite workers from all parts of the railroad industry. A railroad fireman named Eugene V. Debs was elected its president. In April 1894 ARU members went on strike against one of the country's largest railroad companies, the Great Northern of Minnesota, which had also cut wages. After an 18-day strike, the company agreed to go into arbitration. A group of local business owners met with the railroad company's president and Debs. The arbitration panel

23

then decided the company should restore the old wages.

Seeing the success of the Great Northern strike, several thousand railroad workers joined the ARU each day. More than one-third of the workers at Pullman's company joined. On May 7, 1894, members of the union met with Pullman. They complained about the wage cuts and Pullman's refusal to lower their rents. They also pointed out that many foremen still treated the workers unfairly. Pullman refused to consider their demands. He told the workers they should move if they could not afford the rent in Pullman. But workers who lived outside Pullman were often the first to be fired. In addition, residents of the company town were more likely to get promoted than the workers who lived in nearby towns.

Three days later, Pullman fired three of the workers who had made the demands. The next day several thousand Pullman workers came to the factory as usual. But labor leaders at Pullman had already decided the workers should strike to protest the firings. Most workers soon left the

Railway workers were forced to live in shacks during the strike.

factory. Pullman was surprised by the strike. He said, "I believed the men were satisfied with the arrangements." With so few workers available, he shut the factory.

The strike began peacefully on that May morning. Union officials had told the workers to respect the law and not cause trouble. One newspaper reported that everything was quiet in Pullman, with "women, children, and men pass[ing] up and down the avenues enjoying the sunshine." But within weeks, the Pullman strike turned violent in Chicago and beyond.

25

FROM STRIKE TO BOYCOTT

Some Chicago leaders sought ways to end the strike. A group called the Chicago Civic Federation supported arbitration. Its members included Jane Addams, a reformer who worked with poor immigrants in the city. She met with an ARU leader who told her "he was very friendly toward the idea of arbitration." Pullman, however, would not consider arbitration. He disliked unions and did not want labor leaders to think strikes would make him change his ways of doing business.

Pullman found that many Chicago-based

Jane Addams (1860–1935)

railroad managers shared his position. In 1886 those railroad companies had formed a group called the General Managers' Association (GMA). Together, the GMA companies owned 41,000 miles (65,600 km) of track and employed more than 220,000 workers. They agreed to work with Pullman against the ARU.

In June, the ARU held its first national convention in Chicago. By now the union had 150,000 members across the country. The Pullman strike was the main topic at their convention. Some local ARU groups had already decided to boycott any train with Pullman cars—workers refused to load, unload, or run those trains. At the convention, ARU members debated calling a national boycott against Pullman cars.

Striking Pullman workers went to the convention, seeking support for the boycott. One of them was Jennie Curtis. Just 19, she was president of the ARU's "girls" group in Chicago. The teenagers and young women in the girls group sewed the carpets and drapes used in the Pullman cars. Curtis told the convention, "We struck at Mr. Pullman

During the Industrial Revolution, young women and girls often worked in textile factories.

because we were without hope … come along with us, for decent conditions everywhere!"

Eugene Debs was in Chicago for the convention. He feared Pullman would soon start hiring replacement workers if the strike did not end. He also thought most Americans would begin to dislike his union if it called for a boycott. He said, "There is a deep-seated hostility in the country to the term 'boycott.'" Debs feared the young union might not survive the public's dislike of a boycott. Once again, the union tried to see if Pullman would go to arbitration. Once again, he said no.

The workers finally decided a national boycott was their only hope for getting what they wanted. Starting on June 26, ARU workers across the country refused to work as a way to show their support for the Pullman strikers. Within two days, more than 100,000 railroad workers were on strike. A *Chicago Times* headline blared, "NOT A WHEEL TURNS IN THE WEST."

The office of the American Railway Union in Chicago served as strike headquarters.

29

Debs did not want the boycott to become a general strike against all railroads. The main goal was to stop the Pullman cars. But the General Managers Association decided to stir up anger against the union and took steps to hurt it. The railroad companies began hiring out-of-work men to fill in for the strikers. The companies also attached Pullman cars to trains that did not usually pull them, such as freight and mail trains. The railroads hoped that if those trains were boycotted, many Americans would feel the effects and turn against the striking ARU workers. The GMA also hoped that adding the Pullman cars to these trains would make the U.S. government send in troops to end the boycott.

Debs accused the railroad companies of hiring people to stir up violence, hoping the unions would be blamed. He knew many Americans feared unions and the violence that often resulted from strikes. Debs continued to insist that his members avoid aggression and breaking the law. He wanted to keep popular support. But some people in Illinois

An 1894 anti-union cartoon depicted "King Debs" stopping the trains.

who supported the strikers or simply disliked the railroad companies did take action. They forced several trains to stop running, leading Governor John P. Altgeld to respond. He sent in state troops to make sure trains already running were not stopped. With troops on the scene, the threat of violence faded.

THE U.S. GOVERNMENT STEPS IN

President Grover Cleveland was alarmed by the stoppage of trains. The U.S. government had a duty to make sure the mail was delivered and that goods went from one state to another.

Richard Olney (1835–1917)

Richard Olney was the U.S. attorney general, the government's top lawyer. Olney had once worked for several railroad companies. He supported the GMA and wanted to break apart the union, just as the railroad companies did. He knew that Chicago was the center of the strike, so he said, "Whatever was done should be done at Chicago … *if smashed there*, it would collapse everywhere else."

Olney convinced Cleveland to have U.S. courts issue an injunction against Debs and the union. The July 2, 1894, legal action ordered the union to stop its boycott of GMA trains and any trains carrying mail. Cleveland also accepted Olney's wish to send U.S. troops into Chicago. They began arriving just after midnight on July 4.

By this time violence had already broken out in cities nearby, but Chicago itself was quiet. Governor Altgeld was

Soldiers guarded a mail train to keep the angry mobs from attacking it.

upset that the president had acted on his own. Normally the president only sends in troops after a governor asks for help. The trains weren't running, Altgeld said, because the companies did not have enough workers—not because of violence. Newspaper reports of violence, he said, were often lies. In a letter to the president he wrote, "Very little actual violence has been committed." But Cleveland insisted that the troops stay in Chicago, and more soon arrived.

The greatest violence happened after the soldiers came to Chicago. Mobs burned and tipped over railcars, and a security guard shot and killed several men. Train service in Chicago came to a halt, leading to shortages of food in different parts of the country. Violence also spread to other parts of the country, including California, Oklahoma, and Utah. At one point, about 250,000 Americans were on strike, though the number that took part in riots was much smaller.

By the middle of July, some ARU workers began to see that they could not win the strike. George Pullman still

Rioting in the Panhandle train yards in South Chicago resulted in $340,000 in damages.

would not arbitrate, and the public disliked the violence and shortage of goods. Other major unions had refused to join the strike. And it was clear the U.S. government had sided with the railroad companies and would not let the strike go on.

Trains began to run regularly again, and Eugene Debs and several other union leaders were arrested for ignoring the July 2 injunction. On July 18 a sign went up

When the strike ended, wrecking crews cleaned up the damages at Chicago train yards.

at the Pullman Palace Car Company, saying the company
would reopen "as soon as the number of operatives [work-
ers] taken on is sufficient [enough] to make a working force
in all departments." Over the next several weeks, many
of the striking workers came back to the factory. By early
September the *Chicago Tribune* reported that "all labor unions
and the public generally have lost interest in it [the strike]."

AFTER THE STRIKE

While the strike was winding down, the U.S. government began to study what had caused the Pullman strike. It also wanted to know exactly what happened during the strike and boycott. The U.S. Strike Commission questioned workers, military officers, and railroad company officials,

The U.S. Strike Commission consisted of (left to right) U.S. Commissioner of Labor Carroll D. Wright, John D. Kernan, and Nicholas E. Worthington.

37

including George Pullman. The commission said it knew that many business owners and Americans in general disliked unions. Yet given the size and power of companies, unions had a role to play in protecting workers.

The commission suggested that strikes could be avoided if capital and labor had to accept the results of arbitration. Avoiding strikes was especially important with the railroads, since they were vital to the U.S. economy.

The strike led some important Americans to change their thinking about unions. Attorney General Richard Olney now thought that they had value. Workers needed to join together when dealing with capital, which had more power and money than labor. In 1898 he supported a law that addressed many of the strike commission's concerns. The law made it illegal for companies to prevent their workers from joining unions. The law also called for arbitration in railroad disputes that might lead to damaging strikes.

Though the U.S. Supreme Court overturned the law in 1908, these legal changes marked the first time the

In 1922, the United States faced another major strike when 400,000 railway shop workers went on strike. Workers were brought in to replace strikers and keep trains running.

government tried to help labor in its struggle with capital. But many industrial workers were still unhappy. They thought that the use of the military and the courts against them in 1894 proved they could never get a fair deal. The Pullman strike had weakened the power of unions. It took several more decades for labor to win stronger laws that protected its right to strike.

Eugene Debs saw the Pullman strike as a turning point for labor. In 1895 he was sent to prison for six months for his role in the strike. He later wrote that the Pullman strike convinced him workers had to take stronger action against business owners. To do this, Debs formed the Socialist Party of America. It called for the government, not private citizens, to own the factories and for the workers to control them. U.S. Socialists tried to strengthen labor unions as they fought for their goal. Most workers, however,

Eugene Debs was the Socialist Party's candidate for president in 1904.

In 1955, the American Federation of Labor and the Congress of Industrial Organizations merged to create the AFL-CIO, the largest union in the world.

rejected Debs' ideas. They believed Americans should be allowed to own companies, if they could. They simply wanted the government to treat them fairly, instead of favoring capital.

The number of American workers in unions reached its peak during the 1950s. One out of every three workers in private companies belonged to a union. Today about 12 percent do. But unions played a role in giving workers shorter workdays, higher wages, and safer factories. The Pullman strike led Americans to closely examine the relationship between capital and labor in the United States.

GLOSSARY

arbitration—a process of settling a disagreement between two or more people or groups, by a person chosen by them

boycott—a refusal to do business with someone as a form of protest

economy—the way a country produces, distributes, and uses its money, goods, natural resources, and services

injunction—a legal action that requires someone to do or not do something while a judge gathers facts about an issue

leasing—paying money for the right to use something owned by another person or company

riots—large gatherings of people who use violence to show their anger

union—group formed by workers to seek better pay and working conditions

DID YOU KNOW?

- In 1898 the Illinois Supreme Court forced the Pullman Palace Car Company to sell all its property in the town of Pullman that was not needed for company business. All the homes were sold by 1907, and today Pullman is a part of Chicago.

- As leader of the Socialist Party of America, Eugene Debs ran five times for U.S. president. He did best in 1920, when he won more than 900,000 votes.

- During the Pullman strike, 12 people were killed in and around Chicago, and more than 500 were arrested.

- Starting in the 1880s, some unions called for a national holiday to honor workers. After the Pullman strike, Congress passed a law creating Labor Day, which is celebrated on the first Monday in September.

- When Eugene Debs was released from prison in 1895, he was treated as a hero by many workers. About 100,000 people met the train that took him to Chicago.

IMPORTANT DATES

Timeline

1867	George Pullman opens the Pullman Palace Car Company.
1880	Pullman begins building a new town for his workers just south of Chicago.
1886	Pullman workers and others around the country strike in support of a shorter workday.
1893	Pullman's company begins cutting wages and firing workers.
1894	In May, Pullman workers go on strike; in June, the American Railroad Union calls for a national boycott; in July, U.S. troops enter Chicago and riots break out; the boycott ends.
1895	The U.S. Strike Commission issues a report on the Pullman strike, calling for arbitration in future railroad strikes.
1898	Congress passes a law giving workers the right to join unions and calling for arbitration in railroad strikes.

IMPORTANT PEOPLE

JANE ADDAMS (1860–1935)

Reformer who helped immigrants and workers; she founded Hull-House, which provided care for immigrant children and offered language classes to their parents in Chicago

JOHN P. ALTGELD (1847–1902)

Governor of Illinois during the Pullman strike; a German immigrant, he became a lawyer and entered politics during the 1880s

GROVER CLEVELAND (1837–1908)

Twenty-second and 24th U.S. president who ordered troops into Chicago during the Pullman strike; he is the only president to serve two terms not in a row

EUGENE DEBS (1855–1926)

President of the American Railway Union who later founded the Socialist Party of America; he ran for U.S. president five times

GEORGE PULLMAN (1831–1897)

Founder of the Pullman Palace Car Company and builder of the town of Pullman, Illinois; he spent time in Colorado during the 1860s, trying to earn money for his railroad car business

WANT TO KNOW MORE?

At the Library

Benson, Sonia. *Development of the Industrial U.S. Almanac.* Detroit: Thomson/Gale, 2006.

Collier, Christopher. *The Rise of Industry: 1860–1900.* New York: Benchmark Books, 2000.

Laughlin, Rosemary. *The Pullman Strike of 1894: American Labor Comes of Age.* Greensboro, N.C.: Morgan Reynolds, 2000.

Meltzer, Milton. *Hear That Whistle Blow!: How the Railroad Changed the World.* New York: Random House, 2004.

Stein, R. Conrad. *The Pullman Strike and the Labor Movement in American History.* Berkeley Heights, N.J.: Enslow Publishers, 2001.

On the Web

For more information on this topic, use FactHound.

1. Go to *www.facthound.com*

2. Type in this book ID: 0756533481

3. Click on the *Fetch It* button.

FactHound will find the best Web sites for you.

On the Road

Labor History Museum of the
Illinois Labor History Society
28 E. Jackson, Room 1012
Chicago, IL 60604
312/663-4107
Small museum with old books,
photos, memorabilia, and artifacts

Pullman Historic District
11141 S. Cottage Grove Ave.
Chicago, IL 60628
773/785-8901
The only remaining building in
George Pullman's company town

Look for more We the People books about this era:

The American Newsboy
Angel Island
The Great Chicago Fire
Great Women of the Suffrage
*   Movement*
The Harlem Renaissance
The Haymarket Square Tragedy
The Hindenburg
Industrial America

The Johnstown Flood
The Lowell Mill Girls
The Orphan Trains
Robert Fulton's Steamboat
Roosevelt's Rough Riders
Women of the Harlem
*   Renaissance*
Yellow Journalism

A complete list of We the People titles is available on our Web site:
www.compasspointbooks.com

INDEX

About the Author

Michael Burgan is a freelance writer of books for children and adults. A history graduate of the University of Connecticut, he has written more than 100 fiction and nonfiction children's books. For adult audiences, he has written news articles, essays, and plays. Michael Burgan is a recipient of an Educational Press Association of America award.